So Long as We Speak Their Names

So Long as We Speak Their Names

Poems by

Ann Howells

Cover design by Shay Culligan:

Photograph by Ryan Stone

ISBN: 978-1-950462-50-6

Kelsay Books Inc.

kelsaybooks.com

502 S 1040 E, A119
American Fork, Utah 84003

When I recall that small white skiff,
its dove grey trim, I long to wrap myself
in the embrace of faded chambray
you always wore—a lost child without you

Acknowledgments

Apeiron Review: "Now That He Has Died"
Apparatus Magazine: "How Alice Drowned"
Blue Hole: "Cap'n Charlie"
Blue Print Review: "Miss Cora" (as "I do not own my face")
Bohemia: "Terrance"
Boundless (VIPF Anthology): "Cleave,"
The Chaffin Journal: "His House"
Common Ground Review: "Pap Abandons the Church"
Constellations: "Piney Point Marina"
Crannog: "Gone, and Others Like Her," "Sage of St. George"
Dragon Poet Review: "Miss Libby"
Elegant Rage (Woody Guthrie Anthology): "Family Photo"
Emerge: "South River Step and Glide"
Fogged Clarity: "Bastard Speaks"
From Under the Bridges of America (Homeless Anthology):
    "Other Son"
Getting Old Anthology (KY Story): "Miss Frankie"
Glassworks: "Sisters"
Halcyon Days: "Ping"
Halfway Down the Stairs: "Chasing Rabbits"
Houston Poetry Fest Anthology: "Mosquitoes"
Illya's Honey: "Ziggy and the Git Warm"
The Interpreter's House: "Watermen's Wives"
Little Patuxent Review: "Wild Asparagus"
Little River Review: "Tune in Tomorrow"
The Lowestoft Chronicle: "The Cousins Explain Home"
Main Street Rag: "Mavis Farts"
Muddy River Poetry Review: "In the Kitchen of the Big White
    House"
On the Veranda: "Paret, Widowed"
Panoply: "August Bounty"
Poppy Road Review: "In a Secret Place among the Rocks"

Red River Review: "Glorie"
Red Wolf Journal: "Nor'Easter"
River Lit: "Remembering Cherryfield Point"
River Poets Journal: "Last Innocent Summer"
San Pedro River Review: "Cap'n Woodie," "Miss Ruta,"
    "The Night Clerk," "Time and Tide"
Secrets and Dreams Anthology (Lost Towers Press):
    "The Devil He Knows"
Spillway: "Cartwheels," "Twilley Blood"
Surrounded: Living with Islands (Write Wing Press):
    "Waterman's Wife"
Third Wednesday: "Frog Moon, Honeysuckle Moon"
Whale Road Review: "Jo-rie on Deck"

I would also like to thank members of Dallas Poets Community
workshop group for their invaluable input on many of these
poems, their support, and their friendship.

Contents

Time and Tides

Spume Like the Milky Way

The high tide line's a diadem:
tumbled shell and driftwood's silvered bits
set with jellyfish—translucent moonstones,
crystal orbs into which the gypsy gazes,
foretells a coming season.
Tide at its perigee is catatonic,
risen from dint and dimple
to lie flat as a scrying mirror
or museum case displaying pearled shell,
blackened nail, rusted hinge. It lies
among graves in the little churchyard
where loved ones rest, sealed in cement vaults
and hand-hewn caskets
snug as sturdy little boats we trust
to bring us home each suppertime
when nets and dredges are emptied.

Milkweed greens and water willow.
Submerged rock flutters silky maidenhair
and ruffled umber skirts that may
or may not lift
as you take the weathered hand extended,
step lightly into the waiting boat.

Storm Season

Nor'easter

Trees crack, take out their lines,
leave them blinded and mute,
feeling on Grandpa's rolltop desk
for kerosene lamps—
a company of reserves called up
in times of barometric unrest—
when the needle falls,
unease measured
in inches of mercury.

Growling northeast wind
pushes tide, drives whitecaps,
nips heels, herds waves inland,
onto the beach and into yards.

They are in a waterglobe
shaken by an angry child;
horizontal sheets of water—
blend of sea and sky—close over,
deep water engulfs the road,
divides the island.

During brief lulls
grey-green troughs reveal
the pale profile of their boat,
naked pilings—
sentinels derelict in duty.
Their pier is gone, lifted,
ripped away, dashed against rock,
debris to be gathered from sand—
a weed and driftwood edging
that diagrams a high water line
six feet from their door.

Good Old Days

By Thursday
the drawstring purse hung
flat and flaccid,
a third breast on Mama's chest.

Under a bleached sky
brown landscape curling at the edges
they walked slouched shoulders
of domed county roads,
picked up bottles, two cents each,
filled the small, wooden wagon
Capt'n Auty built.

Along twitching marshes
down the beach older brothers
and sisters lay summer evenings
on blankets, drank spiked wine,
initiates in mysteries
they vaguely guessed.

Up around the bridge
fishermen loitered at night
coarse voices rolled out to sea
as men swatted mosquitoes,
scattered small brown bottles,
beer called *little Knicks,*
purchased by the sackful.

Scouring gravel lots
between bars and piers, the boys
culled from detritus: whiskey flasks,
twisted cigarette packs, gum wrappers,
ticket stubs, one high-heeled sandal,
the familiar brown glass.

At Mr. Eddy's store
coins dropped from mired hands,
purchased meal, pea-beans,
sliver of fatback. Friday's supper,
meager, always the same.

Today they get together
over coffee, a beer,
or glass of Chardonnay.
They smile, reminisce
about the good old days.

Mosquitoes

Tires shush on domed macadam
beyond county maintenance—
acres of saw grass, home to crab,
brine shrimp and snake.
Those who crave solitude
seek the salt marsh.

I flee sisters come together
to help the youngest recuperate.
Two days, and old rivalries
bubble up, spoil the broth. So I
return to the point, the familiar
sulfur reek of home.

Heavy, dank air glisters
my windshield. Headlights carve
a cavern deep in country-dark;
mosquitoes swirl toward me
like snowflakes. Were I to crack
a window the car would fill
with high-pitched whine.

Hatchlings float on stagnant pools,
semi-liquid earth; black clouds
swarm at dawn and dusk. Only
the females bite—tiny furies,
striped grey on grey. Their soft bodies
bulge with blood.

Watermen's Wives

Mornings when sky is red, the wives pray. They pray
while baking fish with potatoes and onions,
while walking rutted roads to buy flour, coffee, sugar,
while gathering eggs, scattering feed by handfuls.
Sea pounds and crashes into shore.
Wives pray while they harvest cucumbers, tomatoes
from the little patch beyond the kitchen.
They whisper prayers in church on Sunday
and on knees beside the bed at night.
The wives pray when a boat is christened,
when bass appear on schedule,
when men in slickers and sou'westers
launch themselves into storm,
when workboat engines *putt-putt* shoreward.
Summer folk mouth different prayers.

Camouflage of Words

Impermanence
is the order of the day.
What floats is gone;
what's left is ruined.
Flood waters wail—
terrible arias
resound in my skull.
Voices like gulls
cry over distance:
windblown, faint,
incomprehensible.
Faces pulsate, meld.
Nothing but mud
and stench. Stench
and mud. Debris.
I rely on cousins
of distant cousins,
friendships
many times removed.
I am flotsam.
I am jetsam.

Waterman's Wife

The morning river is enshrouded,
but, still, men search, know time
and tide, divide the waters
with imaginary lines—

Tropic of Duty, Tropic of Concern—
each searches his portion, emerges,
specter from the fogbank, glides
silently past, skiff almost invisible.

The boat has been found,
water-logged and foundering.
Boys pole the shallows, probe reeds
where tide has come and gone.

In the kitchen brood hens cluck,
pat hands, dish up casseroles. But,
she has been in their place, knows
the harbored relief, *it's not my man.*

She slips out, walks the shore
as mist burns off, searches for a break
in the small boats' silent gliding,
in the men's intentness.

Any coming together means
he's been found, surfaced
on this, the third day. They will try
to spare her the belly distended

as though he's feasted, the fluttering
white flesh: fingers, toes, lips fringed
and waving like anemones, eyes gone.
She won't eat crabs for months.

Family Photo

Five of them pose together
with the big, swaybacked mule. Four
ride its back in various animated postures:
three brothers, one sister. Linnie, the eldest,
stands beside. Line and angle. Flat chest.
No hips. Lank hair. Her clothes hang.

She does not want to be there. Notice
the background coop and chicken yard.
Her job: stand at a rough table adjoining
the fence, pump water and wipe shit
from eggs before packing them for market.
She hates it.

Summer folk pass along the rutted road,
smile, say hello. She looks through them,
does not respond, though her cheeks
blaze red.

Saltbox

The big white house on the island,
windows nearly occluded
by waxy pink camellias, old house
built by Grandfather's hands,
whitewashed block, blue-shingled roof,
filled with lessons and laughter.
It is where I return in dreams,
where I once belonged, sand
and saltwater cling to threadroots.
Father is there, whiskery
and complacent, calloused hands
resting on a full belly. Mother
is there, wiry and careworn,
violets on the windowsill,
cats in the pump house.
Apron strings dangle at her sides;
I offer infrequent telephone calls,
frivolous useless gifts,
money she tucks away. One duffle
cannot contain the guilt.

Twilley Blood

I might have stepped
from forehead, his eye,
belly or rib: tousled dark curl,
squared jaw, eyes set in laughter—
suns behind high cheekbones—
so blue the whites seemed tinted.

What I have of Mama came slowly
as I suckled, drank her in.
Mama—foster child,
brothers like out-of-town cousins—
distrusted his large, unruly family.
Damned Twilley blood! she spat,
and, oh, how closely she watched
for foolish notions to develop.

I was like Papa, core of her universe,
yet, therefore, like *them*. Mama
watched me grow with jealous eyes.

Devil He Knows

When he removes the nail
it leaves a small O on his foot,
thorn prick round and red as a leech's mouth.
He doesn't want to be scolded,
so he keeps it secret. Days later
a tender red starburst colors his sole.
He worries at the stink,
yelps when he bumps it. It swells, throbs,
stains his sock a greenish-yellow.
He cushions it with tissue,
steps carefully around Mom and Pop.
But, his sister spies the swelling,
angry and festered, extending from bedclothes,
squeals to Mom who bathes, treats,
takes him to a doctor
who pulls a chromed lamp down close, probes,
says infection has progressed to bone,
prescribes a new drug: expensive.
Pop whips him hard for hiding the wound,
says omission is a kind of lie.
But, a whipping for lying
is no worse than a whipping for carelessness.

Tune in Tomorrow

Darla's husband, Willet,
stands on the front walk, shouts her name,
curses her, the lawnmower, and damp grass
that clogs the blade. Inside,
she cleans a puddle the cat left in the hall,
entertains their daughter, in-laws,
minister, and Willet's mother.
She wipes; Willet curses.
Finally, his mother snatches the rag,
pushes her out the door, straight into the fire.

I think of a time my husband and I argued;
he pulled back a fist, looked at it in shock,
not believing what he might have done. And Willet,
who knows what he might do?
Darla sits beside me, says Willet
bought her a pick-up hitch for her birthday;
year before it was a casting rod.
She speaks of a son so addicted to alcohol
he vomits blood, suffers seizures,
blacks out whole weekends. Another
does four to seven in Folsom. She
picks up a beer, asks if I'd like one,
as if to wash down the embarrassment
of such sudden unburdening.

Other Son

Bosses adore him, until he staggers in
red-faced, clench fisted.
      Step down.
Jobs are hard to find, menial, low-paid,
what with jail time, bad references.
      Step down.
Women who take him home,
find him charming, grow wary.
      Step down.
He seeks acquaintances to offer a bed,
sofa, floor space—family had enough,
friends no longer accept calls.
      Step down.
Nights are bitter, streets a wasteland—
he finds some pals. Lives in his car,
until it's towed.
      Step down.
Three strikes with Salvation Army—
no hits, no runs, no detox—just
bloody vomit, bloody shit, collapse.
      Step down.
Spiral the maelstrom, spinning,
bottom in sight. But, through his haze
it looks like blue sky.
      Step down.

Bastard Speaks

got yer mama's nose
folks say
got her mouth
must be
they fit your knuckles

my coat of colors
fades:
black to purple
blue to green
yellow to brown

i wear battle ribbons
of scar

bastard
you spit
no kid of mine

and your words
bring solace

Cleave

It is not, she says, *that we were
made in the same mold, for we are
not the same. Rather, we were made
in different molds, but of the same
material.*

> silk purse or parachute
> sealing wax or votive
> goblet or mullioned pane
> clamshell or pillar
> macramé or mooring line

Cousins, yes, and more—
connected through some sixth
or seventh sense. Perhaps
twins in a previous life. Perhaps,
a blueprint of each imprinted,
secretly, within the other. Perhaps,
in some great cosmic mishap,
a single soul was split in two.
Then, a mouthful of words
sever the bond forever.

Mavis Farts

…Mavis! Whom our mothers held up
in example from kindergarten on. She
of the black velvet eyes, rose-petal blush,
and natural curl. Who never ate salad
with her dessert fork or spilled cranberries
on the tablecloth. Whom all little girls
wanted to be, and all little boys wanted
to marry. Who had no gawky teen years,
no acne, no braces. Mavis.

Always tasteful. Immaculate. Appropriate.
Who instinctively knew what to say—
what not to mention. Godiva chocolate
wouldn't melt in her mouth! Mavis,
who did not lose her temper, shout
or swear. Whose voice flowed
like warm honey. Who had, somewhere,
acquired a southern accent. Who never
had bed-head, lipstick on her teeth,
or runs in her stockings. Whose bra straps
didn't slip, nails didn't break; who
required no safety pins in her clothing.

Mavis, who didn't have swollen ankles
or morning sickness; who assured us
they were psychosomatic. Who didn't
lose her figure after. Mavis, whom
our mothers praise as they look at us
with resignation, whom old men adore
and young men still look at—twice.

Mavis lost her place at the right hand
of Emily Post when she slipped
into the room, thinking she was alone,
let a long, rumbling fart before exiting
through another door. I couldn't wait
to get back to the reception. Couldn't wait
to tell.

Sage of St. George

An old woman prays. Her words, like beads,
bounce, skitter, roll beneath furniture
as her lips move silently; long brown fingers
point straight to heaven. She seems St. Joan
from my French primer, untouched amid flames
and dressed in white, though she
like all island women wears a much-washed dress
fashioned of feed sacks, smelling faintly of corn.

Our big white house becomes a monkey house,
all *scritch* and *chitter*. Neighbors stuff towels
along sills, place pots where water works in,
make cinnamon toast and tea—
screaming kettle unheard above shrieking winds.
Only the old woman remains focused,
stares down the storm, head unbowed,
body in an attitude of prayer. Tumult swirls
around her. Waves rise, strain forward,
rip at foundations, trees, roof—
dark, wet hands with frothy claws.

Did she appeal directly to God
or simply cluck and coo like the chickens
she raised? I'll never know
if her prayers saved us, or if, as radio reported,
the hurricane simply trekked out to sea.
Months later, at her funeral,
churchwomen sniggered, called her a seer
and a witch, said she'd burn in hell.
It was then, September thirty years ago,
I gave up religion.

Miss Willie

Miss Willie's parents named her
William Eugene . . .

bottlenose dolphin   goggle-eyed scad

how sad she must have been knowing
she was not what they wanted . . .

pot-bellied pig   blue-footed booby

they carry bile beneath their tongues . . .

dung beetle   humpback whale   stink bug

like taxidermists who exaggerate the grotesque
and malformed . . .

warthog   clown fish   three-toed sloth

ensure the glass remains, always,
half empty . . .

hammerhead   walleye   night crawler

puff adder   bardog   mud puppy

The Watermen's Wives Speak

Flora speaks:
> I'm a weed, pure and simple. Bloom where I am.
> Wishful thinkin' ain't gonna make me no steel magnolia.
> Hand pump, andiron, skillet fryin' up scrapple
> n' slumgullion. I'm cast iron. Pies cool on tha sill
> in my red n' white kitchen; stoneware crocks
> line tha wall—I salt down fish all summer,
> dole em' out in lean months

Vadis speaks:
> Hidden beneath my black umbrella I watched Goldie
> lowered into sleety ground, recalled her face trembling,
> distressed, as rain fell on a new grave. *Promise me,*
> she whispered, *you won't bury me in rain.* She
> spoke often of cremation, yet when I asked Willie
> why he didn't follow her wishes. He stared wide-eyed:
> *I never even heard her mention that!*

Lettie speaks:
> I pace my widow's walk; skirts trimmed to the wind,
> boots chamfer planks, heart stutters, startled bird trapped
> within a cage of ribs, poised for flight. Laced corset
> supports broken ribs, ruffled taffeta covers bruises
> faded yellow, salty oceans pour into my wounds as I
> raise my glass to the horizon, see the ship that sails
> roiling nightmares. I finger my crucifix, pray it's not his,
> one that returns a bellow-lunged, mallet-fisted brute.

Hattie speaks:
> I slosh his shirts in suds, rinse, feed through a wringer,
> mindful of my cousin's withered arm. Hand-stitched hems
> snap—flags on a line. Shirts puff—windsocks signaling
> semaphore. I watch others' children at play:

clothespin dolls and seedpod boats, castles in sand.
Beneath a catalpa I fan myself with a funeral home fan.
I'll die, still in this voluminous apron. Stolid.
Complaisant to the end.

Melva speaks:
They dropped, stones from my womb. Cold. Blue.
Never gazed with unfocused eyes into my own.
Barely the size of kittens the barn cat produces,
effortlessly, several times a year—an affront. I felt
pleasure tying them into sacks, adding rocks, tossing them,
mewling, from the pier. But, when a child, a niece,
is found floating, hair haloed around a cherub face,
neighbors look askance, whisper behind my back.

Fannie speaks:
When we met, he called me his pearl, praised
sea-blue eyes, luminescent skin. I'm a slight woman,
tee-shirt and jeans, too rough to be anyone's pearl
till I remember a pearl is just a bit of grit covered
by layer after layer of nacre. I wonder if he suspects
the amount of grit at my center.

Lisbet speaks:
Etched on my heart is a map of this place: every lane,
shack, rusted car. I understand its quaint psychology.
There's Cap'n Lloyd who mounted a telescope
in his front window; Cap'n James buttoned in a sweater
even in summer; and old Miss Cox, first with a casserole
when there's a death. There's Cap'n Haines listing left
from childhood polio, and Miss Adams walking a mastiff
twice her size. There, too, goes that red-headed kid
who delivers groceries, and there's someone I don't know.
I don't like the looks of him.

Glorie speaks:
> When flesh and blood abandoned me—no use
> for a girl child, the willow opened its arms, and I
> found refuge. Now, life has come full cycle;
> I sit again in its sanctuary as amber leaves spill
> into chill October, tide drums mindlessly
> in funeral cadence. My sons worry—crazy way
> to mourn, perched in a tree, watching diggers,
> cement crosses, lichen-stained stones: Mama, Papa,
> now my Bill. Wild cherries bleed upon the ground.
> Never time for explanation, never reason for my boys
> to sit in a comforting tree and weep.

Ruta speaks:
> Dust motes settle like snow on Mama's old Philco,
> angles rounded as if chamfered by time,
> dial a clockface, bulky Bakelite knobs. Hank Williams,
> Eddie Arnold, and the ingenue, Patsy Cline, sang here
> daily. But Saturday night, Mama pulled her chair close,
> listened—imagine, listened—to wrestling,
> cheered Gorgeous George, relived every body-slam
> and count while Papa grumbled it was all fake.

Addie speaks:
> Because I am candid, a chatterbox, you assume my life
> splays before you like my legs, banquet on white linen:
> meat and go withs—sweet and savory—for you
> to feast upon, but no. I offer you *what, where,* and *who,*
> and you are unaware I keep *why* to myself, some parts
> of me will never be yours. I stare at the ceiling,
> inky blackness turning grey.

Mae speaks:
> Blind to fishermen lining the rail, beer at hand,
> tackle boxes at foot, casting long lines into the bay.
> Deaf to teens who push and shove, execute
> perfect swan dives, jack knives, cannonballs,
> ignoring hoots and catcalls. On this narrow beach,
> I sit, stare across sun-sequined water you loved.
> Tide gently laps my feet, washes in, washes out.
> I am alone as I will ever be; long to feel your arm
> about my shoulder.

Nola speaks:
> . . . when tha sewer come through, she dint have
> no money—county say they take it from her es-tate.
> Now her ass be settin' on porcelain . . . never had
> no indoor plumbin' her whole life. Miss High Yella
> settin' pretty now. Her mama regal like that Nefertiti,
> long back like some kinda cat. Ole Charlie,
> done picked hisself a good'un. Right smart lookin'
> when he young—trim hips, flashin' daddy's money,
> dint have no trouble gettin' wimin, white or black
> dint make no difference. But, he treat that chile
> like she sumpin', and damned if she ain't, Lily,
> damned if she ain't.

Lena Speaks:
> Wind riffles the hydrangea in listless sighs,
> and rain treks my cheeks. In the kitchen's
> still green air I chop carrots, turnip, onion.
> Soup is the flavor of settling in, latching shutters,
> lighting fires. Words lodge in my throat

41

like marrow in bone—fat, flavorful,
enriching the stock. I move with practiced ease
through domestic chores, bubble of stew a heartbeat,
biscuits on the plate a still life. He's gone five weeks;
calendar pages drift like leaves.

Sturdy Peasant Stock

The world turns monochrome,
grey on grey of old daguerreotypes.
He shakes his head—
he's been through flood, hurricane,
and worse on this island.
He brings oil lamps from the attic,
draws buckets of water.
He's eighty-eight, his wife blind.
Still, she was a waterman's daughter,
navy widow, all sinew and gristle.
Landline goes, then electricity.
She uses her cell phone sparingly—
checks in with the kids
morning and night—till it too dies.
Bundled in jackets and heavy socks,
they eat peanut butter and cheese,
nibble Oreos, tell stories in the lamp's
dim penumbra. Every minute
echoes the previous;
they fret only about propane tanks
washed against the house.

They were ordered to evacuate,
the fire department tells his son,
but the couple makes do—
they've made do all their lives—
remain in that little cottage
inside the water globe
till volunteers arrive, remove tanks,
bring them a special treat—
thermos of hot coffee.

Moving Day

It was time. It was past time.
But he sure hated to go
into that place. *Assisted Living,*
his nephew called it,
but it was the *Old Folks Home.*
Two crowded rooms
instead of his big old house.
Well, he'd been living
mostly in three rooms anyway—
bedroom, kitchen, sun porch.
Bent almost double
with arthritis, couldn't hear
a damn thing, and his glasses
magnified like binoculars.
He just needed more care
than the county nurse could give
in her daily visit, and his nephew,
well, the young man
had to earn a living, didn't he?
He'd signed the house
over to him when he moved in
three years ago, had to do it
or the county'd take it.
You got to be poor
to get in the county home,
but he'd sure miss
sitting on the sun porch,
gulls squalling,
workboats lumbering past,
little skipjacks skimming the waves.
He'd lived on this island
all his life, he always thought
he'd die here.

How Alice Drowned

Sunset melded lavender-blue,
into ever-deepening indigo.
It was Sunday,

a soft evening when
gossamer wings might carry her
all the way to the moon

and back. Her hair drifted,
swayed gently as anemones in tide,
and moonlight covered her

in sequined scales. She
allowed herself to descend,
lured by the oysters' joyful song.

Breath by Breath

Earth exhales and mists rise—
spidery hands etch pines, piers.
Moored boats materialize
while islanders disappear:
diluted blood, assimilated names.

I've read of Pangaea,
seen seashells atop western mesas,
and this island, my island,
haloed by reeds,
seaweed crowning the tide line,
is neither continent nor country.
Seas nibble it thinner;
sands travel marauding tides.
Horizons glow gold,
peach, rose, and palest orchid,
but even now,
a new hurricane brews in the gulf.

Piers and Anchors

Conjuring the Chesapeake

Like charms jangling a bracelet,
whispered incantations:

Accokeek
Aquasco
Chickanuxen
Monokin
Nanjemoy
Nanticoke
Pocomoke.

Little white-washed towns,
villages,
named in the Piscataway tongue—
morning sky blushing red,
and rushing, tumbling rivers:

Choptank
Patuxent
Potomac
Wicomico—
Assateague Island.

This history I lock away,
bury deep
in the vault of consciousness,
sifts through fingers of my mind,
a miser's gold coin.

In a Secret Place among the Rocks

a mound of butterflies stunned
by sudden chill huddle, wings misted damp.

Moss carpets humus-rich forest floors,
vast miniature forests—tiny lives lived out
among virgin timber barely one-inch tall.

Creeper vine and honeysuckle, sun-seekers,
stretch along telephone lines; fern unfurls
between water smoothed stones.

I'd forgotten this, and little locusts springing
like dandelions, topiary kudzu-shapes,
trees so tall, everything green, green, green.

Old settlements and waters labeled long ago
speak the Piscataway tongue: Nanjemoy,
Accokeek, Potomac, Patuxent, Chesapeake.

I remember though the big white house
at the center of the world, kettle simmering,
doors flung wide.

Cap'n Charlie

Sitting on the riverbank,
he extends a rough, brown hand,
reveals, nestled there, an intricate
domed mosaic—numbers crevices
and translucent amber ridges
glowing as if from within.

A tiny drawbridge lowers,
neck telescopes, carved-shell eyes
in a bulbous head, spotted black
on gold like a jungle cat. Trust
thus established, a blade-like tail,
four spotted feet appear.

This great bruin of a man,
lifts a thick finger, displays
within the sanctuary of his hand,
a tiny foot, fine curved claws,
each with a heart of pink vein.
Then bends, gently releases
the terrapin to the waters.

Remembering Cherryfield Point

Miss Paret girded herself
in a blue jacquard bathing suit,
thick and heavy as a wool blanket
above blue-veined legs, only once
or twice each summer. She waded out
knee deep and stopped, rimless glasses
unspotted, grey hair, plaited and coiled,
completely dry. We were not allowed
approach as we swam and splashed.

For exactly one hour she simply sat,
mouth holding neither pins nor clothespins,
hands holding no crochet hook, no
threaded needle. No steaming kettle.
No heated iron. No soapy mop.
She remained, staid and stolid, speaking
when spoken to, admonishing
when we ventured too deep.

Her eyes reflected sun-leached skies.
Her thin lips pressed a firm straight line,
informed us that this hour of idleness
was a grave concession.

Cicadas Provide the Soundtrack

for summer, one-note overture
to morning, predict yet another scorcher.
Big yellow grasshoppers clatter.
Plump red tomatoes hang heavy, corn is tall,
and zucchini have passed their zenith—no longer
do they leave heaping baskets on every porch.
The mosquito truck rumbles rutted lanes,
aims its noxious mist at salt marsh, field, and wood.
Women slam sashes, while children jig
like skeletons in the swirling cloud.
Still cicadas sing a roundelay of wordless praise.
They praise a brassy sun smoldering leached skies
and heat that rises from sandy soil.
They praise workers slick with sweat, kerchiefs
tied about heads, chigger-bit arms and legs,
well-oiled scythes leveling wizened grasses
that rustle and whisper among themselves.
But the cicada's time is almost done;
September approaches, cool evenings
and vespers of crickets beneath the porch.
Grandmothers abandon roiling kettles; mason jars
of peaches, figs, and piccalilli line their shelves—
winter sustenance—as they settle
in rocking chairs, fingers busy with crochet,
the hook's familiar choreography,
muscular memory sufficient
when cataract-dimmed eyes no longer see.
The rocking of their chairs is the ticking of a clock;
invisible shrouds flutter around them.
Ruth and Paret and Ida pass beyond vision,
scatter feed, tend vegetables and children,
prayer books in apron pockets.

No carved headstones weigh them down.
Life swirls past us at the speed of time.
Change does not teeter the horizon
but washes over us in a flood.

After the War

Mosquito truck thunders past,
children dance in billowing poison
as it chuffs the rutted lane.
Inside Althea pencils a line up her leg,
simulates stockings still hard to come by,
clips on rhinestone earrings.
She's grilled cheese for dinner,
with canned tomato soup—
enough for her and mama.
Quick. Easy.
In the yard windfall apples rot;
chickens peck maggots.
Grapes hang heavy; birds'll get 'em soon.
Best pick on Monday if there's to be jelly,
but tonight,
tonight she's going dancing.
There's gas to reach the Brass Rail,
get home. Six dollars in her purse.
If she's lucky she'll buy
only the first rum and coke,
jitterbug all night if a sailor likes to dance,
if he don't get handsy.

She looking for a good time, yeah,
but for a good man too.
Somebody exciting, somebody going places—
places they sing about on radio:
Sioux City, Chattanooga, Kalamazoo—
not island boys up before dawn,
asleep by nine,
mole encrusted by forty,
cataract-glazed by fifty, boys
who'll never leave this goddamn island.

South River Step and Glide

There's a common blood that flows,
taint of salt pulling them to water's edge,
where they take to boats, raise nets dripping
tiny bull's eyes that widen and disappear.
The sun cracks one sleepy eye, peers across
still-darkened surface where boys pole,
skim silently, leaving barest wake,
way Christ must have walked on waters.
They have the same gentle touch, these boys
wiry and brown as cones that litter
beneath island pines, bodies sturdy as
little skiffs they pole. They graze shallows,
scan morning mist and green water for slightest
movement, glimpse of dark green shell,
twirl netted pole *swipp,* break surface
with a hushed *swish,* net a fat peeler
half-buried in sea grass, raise and drop him
to scurry and scramble in the basket,
clack at his fellows. And, the boys pole on,
follow the shoreline, call to others who emerge,
vanish, glide like osprey in morning's half-light,
eye always alert, swooping down for hidden
jimmy or sook. With raptor's grace, muscled
as occasional eel or bar dog they disturb,
they glide in and out of mist as it burns away.
Young, lithe, they harvest the sea, absorb quiet
through their skins, revel in peace and solitude
here, at world's perimeter, knowledge and skill
unquestioned, just *plink* of dripping pole,
swish of net, and *skritch* of crabs as the basket
fills to overflowing.

Wild Asparagus

Don't ask me to explain
differences between roadside
discoveries and market produce.
Ask instead if it seduces me:
path to weed, chigger-thick,
tick infested. Ask if I think
of corn snakes, copperheads
as I push aside grasses,
seek tender crowned stalks.
Ask if I flush bob-whites
startle them to mad run,
my heart to wild pounding.
Ask if I step further, further
tear trousers, mar arms
with bloodied alphabets.
Ask me how the stalks lie
delicate, pale upon my plate,
glisten with butter.

August Bounty

She hugs the waxed carton,
welcomes chill
that penetrates her thin T-shirt
as she trudges sweaty and barefoot
from the store.
Long blackberry canes arch
across the lane,
fruit fat and tantalizing.
Unable to resist, she gorges,
steps deeper,
deeper into undergrowth,
not thinking chiggers or foxes
or snakes,
arms and legs bloodied
with hieroglyphics,
hands and mouth purpled,
milk sitting roadside
slowly going sour.

Pap Abandons the Church

It's that new minister, Father Thomas
he wants to be called. Mr. ain't good enough
for him. High church. Papist. All that
mumbling at the altar; you've no idea
what he's saying. Can't trust a minister
who don't speak out. Verlinder, now,
she can go if she wants; her brothers do
and their wives. That's OK, but I don't
hold with all that folderol. God
can hear me fine, down on my knees
beside the bed.

Father Thomas, harumph,
always got his hand out for charity.
Well, that's OK too, for widows
and orphans, but a man? A man needs
to be supporting his family. If he's got
too many mouths to feed, he should of
kept it in his pants a time or two.
I mean, if a man needs, I'll help.
I don't mind fixing things, tinkering's
a God given gift. But, I'm pretty sure
God don't hold with laziness. Just like
He don't hold with drinking: tried it
once, wasn't worth the morning after.
Wasn't worth the night before neither.
Yep, I'm pretty sure God don't hold
with that. Or with smoking. Or gambling.
It's right there in the Bible. Don't need
no man in a fancy dress to tell me that.

Quiet Woman

she know sumpin
but she don say nuthin
her mouth, it don move
her lips, they don part
her tongue don wag none

yeah, she know sumpin
keep it locked up
in vault of her chest
in well of her throat
in that secret place
'neath her tongue

she know sumpin alright
jus lookit her lettle smile
her oh-so-secret smile
mouth curlin at the corners
make a shallow cup
cradle all them words

but she don say nuthin

Despite the Odds

Ruta keeps a painting of her husband
above the bookcase in her bedroom—
a painting they couldn't afford, but Arnie
had to have one when that travelling artist
came round. It's a good likeness, brings back
good times, before cracked linoleum,
collapsed porch, leaky roof. Before
he drowned—opinion of his seamanship
over-inflated as his opinion of himself.
Blackberry canes arc toward sunlight,
scratch her rusted Ford. Pop music drifts
from her radio, behind windows
propped with rulers or wooden spoons
to catch a puny wind. Painted planks
blister and peal. Weathered saltboxes
scatter among pines. She's been a widow
a long time. She smiles at the painting—
that Arnie had the most devilish grin!

Miss Libby

Her kitchen cathedral,
incense of clove and cinnamon;
jellies line her shelves—
amber and emerald,
      crimson and plum—
stained glass glow.

Family table is an offering;
sweet and savory
      in ideal proportion:
cruet of olive oil,
font of iced tea.

She hums *Old Rugged Cross,*
bends, rolls dough,
      wipes her forehead
      with an apron hem,
crimps with deft fingers
never idle for devil's play.

Scrubbed floor gleams
      its soft patina smoothed
      by countless treads,
soft leather soles.

At the backyard line—
      red, swollen knuckles
      aching with cold—
      she hears confessions.

Dusk at Piney Point

An incandescent sun
bleeds slowly into the river,
stains whitewashed planks
and narrow rails
of the clackety wooden bridge
that flakes paint
onto our blue-shingled roof.
Tide ebbs, beaches re-emerge,
and a workboat putt-putts by
riding low in the water,
hold filled with croakers
and rockfish.
The burning sun dips deeper
into still green water.
Mosquitoes roil from marshes,
and the aroma of spot
fried-up in iron skillets
hovers in still air.
Snore of cicadas ceases.
Lights wink out
in sun-blistered cottages
where berry-brown children
grow lengthy as evening shadows.

Jo-rie on the Deck

Frogs that slept all day, wake and sing
songs of thanksgiving for blood-fat mosquitoes,
swarming gnats, and water-walkers.
They roll up sticky tongues
and pump the bellows of their lungs.
Jo-rie's lighter makes a small flame,
cherries her Marlboro. She sighs.

Jo-rie is on the deck, chores done;
sun-scented sheets in her basket,
doves nodding on the line. *All
is right,* she says, *with the world.*
I hear her pace, back and forth,
back and forth, too restless to sit.
Come see, she whispers at the window;
I slip outside.

Twilight watersnakes pair on the lawn.
Bodies half-erect, they sway hypnotically,
undulate, entwine in their atavistic ritual.
Beautiful, she sighs,
crushes out her cigarette. Bats flit,
like dragonflies, before the moon.

Pines stand shoulder to shoulder
against the dark. A tardy sandhill crane
ripsaws low above the estuary.
*Where was Annie when the lights
went out?* Jo-rie teases. *Where?* I ask.
In the dark! An old joke, and we giggle
longer than it deserves. A nightbird calls,
Jo-rie. Jo-rie.

The Cousins Explain Country

In the city, people
cannot hear you. Their ears
fold closed; their tongues
are clipped.

There, consonants bounce
and tumble, clatter the walk;
you're pressed against bricks,
mouth a silent O . . .

mouth, not voice.
You have no voice,
barely exist, mere reflection
in shop windows.

Here, everyone who enters
is family or friend—
windows spill laughter
and doors are flung wide.

If you walk away, tires hiss
the freeway, windows blink,
doors crack. Turn back,
the pathway is familiar.

Rush to your lighted home
evening after evening;
let bare feet slap the planks.
Let nothing detain you.

Cap'n Woodie

Men still stalk the pines with shotguns,
reeds with netted pole. The river
is a smoked mirror, and mist clings
like fingers of the dead.

While trucks sweep the domed road:
gun racks behind seats,
six-packs in coolers, forty miles
to anywhere, red letters on the marquee
spell out his name. He turns 92 today.

> When young, he tucked
> jars of shine among oysters
> delivered to the capital,
> argued waterman's rights,
> cried out for justice.

His children are in Richmond, Dallas.
He remains, a lower county denizen,
hears bob-white's two note call:
Po'folk. Po'folk. Pine pollen
gilds his world with fool's gold;
it is enough, more than enough.

Gone, and Others Like Her

we recognize paint that curls from whitish
once whitish flanks, copper eroded keel
salt-spitting slash with every storm
sea numbs, skins heaving planks

exposed to grey-green water's scour
she steels herself for lingering death
barnacle and worm invade rotting freeboard
buoys sound her death knell

gaping ribs hold crab, brine shrimp
wavelets pulse like twitching nerves
microcosms flourish in her fractured hull
but a heart beats within her cavernous ribcage

age-ruptured, not quite slipping under
what does slant of abandoned deck tell us
salt-caked windows, muck-sunk stern?
sea will not swallow her whole

noon spreads napalm on the shallows
tidal pool mirrors her—pristine
not derelict, not sunk, not salvage
calloused hands once knew her name

Piney Point Marina

The river, flat and somber,
closed for the season.

Summerfolk are gone:
sleek polished boats,
sleek polished faces.

Pop music no longer
flutters crisp, white curtains.   .

At Evan's Seafood,
two old watermen eat—
oyster stew and saltines.
They do not speak,
allow even this rustic décor
to fade into battered table,
scuffed linoleum, bent-backed wife—
three years gone—filling his bowl
from a simmering kettle.

Eyes look beyond
a quiet Patuxent ebbing
to Chesapeake, to Atlantic,
skim on skipjack-sails
toward a sun that bleeds
into the sea.

Impatience Plucks His Sleeve

He beaches his boat; she'll winter ashore
this year, turned on her back,
a tortoise—plastron exposed

to winter wind, lachrymose winter sun,
drying out even as he must dry out,
give up the Old Crow

which gets him through. There'll be work:
scrape mountainous barnacles from the hull,
check for rot, reseal the bottom

with thick red copper before returning her
to the bay. But oystering is young man's work—
bones penetrated by knife-sharp wind,

balance tested by rough sea, beard caked
with ice. Winter hits, a one-two punch. Brittle
brown kudzu drapes fences like nets

laid to dry. He's not spent so many days
in company of women since he was a child,
but arthritis gnaws his joints, back stiff

as old rope—still he gazes seaward. A rime
of spindrift edges piers, crab shacks,
rip-rap, like old dogs greying

at the muzzle. Even the snow plough
has slipped; men in bulky jackets, knit caps
and gloves, wrestle it

from the ditch. Grey is the color of the day.
His wife, fingers blue from hanging laundry,
tosses a teabag in her constant cup,

pours water from the simmering kettle,
clasps the cup in two hands. *Tea,* he scoffs,
and adds another measure of Old Crow

to his coffee. Impatience plucks his sleeve.
He's useless as gills on a cat, he thinks. *Gills.*
On a damn housecat.

Ping

We hear it at night
ping . . . ping, then a rifle shot
that signals ice is breaking.
It's been years
since this river last froze like this,
Cherryfield to Hell's Point,
skaters crossing shore to shore,
ears nipped raw, breath hoary
on double wrapped scarves
that flap wool-warm shoulders.

Heavy tide fractures the frigid surface,
planks sized like table tops
wrestled onto terra firma, like dinner plates
stacked when mama clears supper.
Sueded skies predicting snow
are warmer, more comforting
than this brilliance:
boats and piers transformed by spindrift to crystal,
pines tinkling like windchimes,
and the air, piercingly bright,
searing exposed fingers,
dazzling eyes blind.

Time and Tide

Mist is silver stillness, a kind of quiet
you can't find in the city.
Objects appear charcoal sketches

on silk; it reflects my mood,
outsider looking in. Here,
in this local restaurant, two old men

sit in contemplation of breakfast.
It is not a morning for conversation.
A young woman in red sleeveless top

and jeans refills my coffee, silent as fog
at the window. Silver starfish in her ears,
rubber sandals on her feet, she looks

to be an islander: mud-colored eyes,
dark hair, staccato speech as if
her mouth is so infrequently used

that once open words gush. I ask
where to rent a boat. She gazes
at the ceiling as if the answer will appear,

message in a magic 8-ball. *Jackie B
rents for parties, but if it's fishing
you want, folks fish right off*

the bridge. She gestures. *It's lit up nights,
and spot are biting real good.*
I contemplate the string-bound box

that rests on my floorboards. He was always an island boy. Perhaps the bridge will serve if I catch the tide just right.

Seeing Pap's Ghost

I awoke when he entered
as when I was a child:
through the stairway door
in denim overalls and socks,
carrying heavy workboots
so as not to wake me.

I'd no reason to fear this man
who gently tolerated,
taught when he could,
enjoyed me best from afar.
He carried heavy workboots
so as not to wake me,

headed for his room above
the porch where blueprints,
drafting tools, lamp with
green glass shade awaited—
through the stairway door
in denim overalls and socks.

Pins and needles tingled flesh,
again and again, till morning
as I lay, lightning struck,
on this anniversary of his death.
I woke when he entered
as when I was I child.

I Been Down

I'm a county girl, and I been down
to the river. Grew up hearin' whispers, yeah,
and sometimes not so quiet:

> *Usin' them big words, don't nobody unnerstand.*
> *Think she sumpin' on a stick!*

Me? I was jus standin' on hot macadam,
shiftin' foot to bare foot, waitin' for the bookmobile,
checkin' out everything they'd let me.

> *That girl! Always got her nose in a book!*

Ladies down at the Methodist Church
thought me strange, but I was there every Sunday.
Besides, I was Woodie's girl. They'd known Woodie
all their lives, so they overlooked a lot.

> *Dorothee Ann! Dorothee Ann!*

They called me by both names cause Grandma did,
even when I done nothin' wrong. I grew up there,
where men were up before dawn, and women
earlier makin' biscuits, fryin' up bacon.

Ain't got money for meat, we make do
  with bass fer dinner. Steamed crabs. Oysters.

I grew up, went to college, but never lost my accent.
I'm still county, an island girl. I belong
same as gulls in the sky, rabbits in the grass,
and, yes, big river rats along the rip rap.

  Me and you, we gotta be real: ain't no Eden
  without a snake.

His Daughter Leaves the Island

Day flares, blazes and consumes itself;
winds shift, and evening's slow air
brings whatever relief will be offered.
She observes her father's long gaze
fixed on the horizon where sea and sky
become indistinguishable.
She understands the sea is his mistress,
not dependable and steady like a wife,
but tempestuous, given to fits and sulks.
Her father's weariness is palpable, his
life governed by tide and season,
by bent back, burnt skin, icy beard,
and chance—crabs, fish, oysters,
each in their time like her, her sister,
her brother, wherever he might be.
She hears quiet resignation when
her dad sighs; he is already thinking
of tomorrow. The sea demands its due.

She kisses his whiskered cheek,
slips into her Honda, waves
till he passes out of sight.

Time and Tides

Off the Map

The map that takes me back along the Chesapeake
is not one my glove box contains,
worn creases and ragged margins marking latitude
and longitude—height, that is, and width.
I'd need a third or fourth dimension to reach
that state between present and rutted lane
where I run bare-soled
dust-powdered-feet on pine-needle carpets,
tar bubbling county-maintained road in August sun.
I hop foot-to-foot beside a ticking marsh to cool the scorch,
swing from wild cherry boughs,
drowse hours belly down on the pier as minnows dart,
dig the dump unearthing funny-old-bottles,
harvest wild asparagus and blackberries,
help G'ma pick grapes *one for the pail, two for me*
or persimmons *yuk, none for me,*
stall forever amid pines' long-needled perfection,
sharp prick of the half-buried cone,
canvas sandals parked under kitchen table.
I pass through the latch-gate,
fence sagging with fuchsia sweet pea,
peepers in the walnut,
blacksnakes in pump-house floor,
mud-daubers in rafters,
not even a shift as earth slows, stops
turns in reverse.
I walk down Thomas Road past crab shacks,
nickel in the cooler for a lemon pop,
cadge a fat slice of Aunt Nora's rhubarb pie,
cross the humpback bridge—
summer cottages alive with cityfolk.
where somebody reminds:

Yer granny gettin' supper 'bout now. . .
I'm running late, but I don't care;
G'ma serves up pandowdy or blackberry slump all the same.
It's just me and Jo-rie, pushing a small world's perimeters,
slipping the map's fine red lines—
tiny lettering naming hamlets long ago absorbed
into a present not half so sweet
as what we've left behind.

Last Innocent Summer

We lived in the willow's cool
green shade—too old to clamber rocks
or gather periwinkles or chase rabbits
on the soft, forest floor. A neighbor
called us *brown as bears.* Others called us
wild as killdeer, but our grannies called us
baby and *darlin', honey* and *dumplin'.*
Cap'n Auty took us to the marl bank,
let us cuddle newborn kittens. Scribby
gave money for nickel slots, taught
about stills. Tink told jokes we did not
understand and leered. Our grannies
raised us: Miss Ruta—seer, healer,
staunch Roman Church; Miss Paret—
staid, Protestant, with the crow's habit
of pilfering shiny trinkets. Nightly
they tumbled us weary into bed;
Jay in an iron bedstead, second floor,
family saltbox, and me in my narrow cot
in the cottage kitchen. We dreamed
of mimosa blossoms, terrapin shells,
and black-veined dragonfly wings,
childhood enfolding us one more year.

Rites

Miss Ruta gentles the rooster,
Old Pecky, who guards his harem
flapping wings and pecking legs.
She coddles him against sagging breasts,
calms him with murmurings,
places him mesmerized on the stump,
and, with a single hatchet flash,
severs his head. It lies, small,

unbloodied, crenellated comb engorged,
black eye bright with accusation
while the body, rough-feathered, indignant,
inscribes crazy circles, jaunty yellow spurs
in mute tarantella across the graveled drive,

scattering droplets like rose petals at a wedding,
smoke at a funeral, salt on the tongue.
At last he topples, and I, acolyte,
sorcerer's apprentice, initiate to the old woman,
trail at her heels like a pup, a goose,
a spring lamb—brown legs embellished
with blood like eastern potentates
with rubies. I am baptized,
will never be innocent again.

Sisters

Comingled blood, dark as windfall cherries, spattered
lichen-streaked stones: grandfather
(dead of foolishness), still-born Baby Anne—
your family plot. And you might have sprung,
angle and bone, from that corner yew, dark,
with dark lank hair. I was summer folk,
mere city girl—pudgy, pale, whiskey-colored ringlets.
But on that garland branch we pricked thumbs,
became sisters.

Envy grew green as island pines.
I was captured by your narrow saltbox:
high-ceilinged rooms, chamber pots beneath iron beds,
stone-floor kitchen with hand pump
and black, wood-burning stove—matriarchal dragon
dominating the room. Your grandmother,
brown and bony as yourself, *knew things*.
I trotted behind as she gentled Sunday's chicken.
Ax arced, shell-carved eye stilled while deranged feathers
convulsed in dervish whirls. I was baptized in blood.
You hungered only for trolley rides,
glass revolving-doors, luncheons on the mezzanine.

Then—one umbrella step ahead as always—
you turned fifteen and left for New Orleans,
a married woman.
Island wives lashed tongues, raised long, red welts
on your memory: *Got herself in trouble. Uh-huh.*
But it wasn't love, or even lust, that lured you;
it was city lights.
If I'd been offered spells or incantation,
I'd have gone too.

Cartwheels

That night at the carnival,
you turned cartwheels
the whole length of the pier—
on a dare—
won five dollars from a boy
on a motorcycle.

Your father left that year
for Knoxville, St. Louis, somewhere—
no use for a girlchild.
You just laughed, moved on,
married young, left for Biloxi,
had three boys: Davie, Zeke and Paul.
Divorced. Married again.
Divorced. Married. Divorced.

Though I remember you,
a young girl cartwheeling,
whenever I pass a roadside carnival,
a narrow vacant pier,
I no longer know your name,

So, if you stumble upon
my address,
torn from an old envelope
and stuck between pages of a book,
write. Say you are
still filled with derring-do,
still the girl I want to be;
spin me tales of bayou life.
But if life has beaten you,
if you are bitter or resentful—
just lie.

Elizabeth and Woodrow

Visitors remember crab cakes and she-crab soup,
laughter and song floating,
windows propped with wooden spoons.
But there's more,
a husband and a wife who came before,
five sons, three daughters, buried.
The past lies gently in the past;
both understand *what if* is a path to discontent.
So scratch cards sprawl the kitchen table,
and radio plays all day.
She spoils him with butter-crust pies
and sugar cakes;
he spoils her with Bingo games and song.
Though hair greys, though knees stiffen,
they dance.

Glorie

The dining room reeks of hot grease,
checkerboard floor cries for a broom,
speaker snaps and buzzes, but the waitress
responds—picks up our plates:
ham and cheese on rye, pickle spear, chips.

Second cousin or first cousin once-removed,
she pretends not to recognize me.
I play along. Make-up cracks
her mouth's corners, furrows plunge
between her eyes, and crayon red hair
reveals mousy roots.

I remember her, all pouty lips and curl,
cut-off jeans, poised atop the arched bridge,
daring boys to dive after her. She tugs
her uniform, too short, too tight;
pours coffee thick and bitter
as herself.

Crab Picker

Peggy Gene rises in still dark night,
fries thick-sliced ham and eggs,
stirs grits, lays out biscuits and jam
for Crowe, on the water before dawn,
laying nets. She wakes the kids,
packs brown bag lunches, kisses them
off to school, reports to the crab shack.

First run is in. Smitty's placed busters
and peelers in boxes, sandwiched soft crabs
in layered sea weed, tossed the rest
in a big pot. Twenty minutes
turns moss green shells a fiery red.
He empties a steamer onto the table;

girls bend heads to their solitary task—
freeing white flesh from shell, packing
pint tins. Since age fourteen.
April through October. This
is what she knows, the way it will be
till arthritis takes her hands,
cataracts steal her sight.

All That Glitters

Midst of hellish August,
ice glitters—if Amie squints,
she can see herself in Amsterdam,
diamond district, wafting sweet tulip smell,
not this fish reek that does not wash away.
She looks past the magnolia,
past pier and rivermouth. On a far shore,
fishermen in black waders wrestle a seine
heavy with frantic squirming flesh—
bountiful catch. Cap'n Rollie sets his scale;
silver girls stand by, filet knives sharp.

Stop dreamin' snaps Lena,
'fore ya lose a finger. But Amie
moves robotic, her hand sure.
Wooden crates teeter on salt-stained planks
grey as Lena's hair, rough as her skin.
Backaches and arthritis slow her. Amie
won't let that happen, but she's uneasy,
twenty already, and no way out.
She gazes at the summer folk, spoiled
or stupid, or both. Still, tears of envy
glitter Amie's eyes.

Miss Goldie

She's drowning like Ahab
tied to the belly of a Great White Hope,
living now on the Chesapeake
where everyone knows her name
if not her face.

Followed her pie-eyed piper
San Angelo to St. Mary's—
pie in the sky.

Now, she runs in place—
place she's known in summer,
learning its winters. Wave action
stacks ice like plates at a buffet.

River bottom muck, marshland reek,
mosquito, tick, moccasin and snapper.
Like an oyster, she summons
bits of grit, creates a pearl.

Miss Cora

All through the family album she finds herself
with upswept curls, ruched-lace collar, bustle.
There, again, in flapper dress, long beads, bob:
high cheekbones, one peaked brow, square jaw,
and eyes of grey or blue, hazel or chocolate brown.
They people an island, a county,
sail down the centuries, indomitable,
white-winged vessels skimming the water.
Where, a daughter asks, *did you get
that picture of my mother?*
The cousin's reply, *That's my mother!*
Every generation: Twilley blood will out.

Common blood. Dominant genes.
Granite-willed women with wide child-bearing hips.
They draw strength from their oneness;
even the names recur: Mae and Annie, Dorothy
and Elizabeth. Bloodline single and twisted
as honeysuckle that masses their fences,
their graves. Just as unstoppable.

Frog Moon, Honeysuckle Moon

Sisters on the pier, legs dangling
brown as mother's mahogany suite,
they are reflective as her stemware.
Sturdy sister, wiry sister—sunburned,
chigger-bit, shin-scraped. Sisters
who hoe a row, shotgun a rabid skunk,
chink windows against storm. Sisters
who make snow angels in sand,
sponge fevered children, watch water snakes
exotic mating dance under a blue moon.

Sisters lullabyed by frog chorus—so resonant
neither hears the other speak, sisters
who have walked morning mists,
solitary and sobbing, followed a shoreline
in soggy slippers. Sisters who share wine,
pass a bottle, too weary to trouble with glasses.

Sisters who read, sisters who write. Sisters
who bury journals in ironing baskets,
tampon boxes, beneath company linens.
Sisters who speak of mother with tolerance,
pity, chagrin. Mismatched sisters,
bound by honeysuckle and poison oak,
flesh pierced by boat hooks and gaffs,
pulled and pressed by tides.

Chasing Rabbits

Our old dog trots to yard's end
barks at a helmeted cyclist and passes
unaware within six feet of a rabbit
who wears immobility
like an invisibility cloak.
The rabbit knows the dog is blind—
right eye a milky blue
left one dim beneath a sheen
like oil on water. The rabbit nibbles
crocus and sprouts beneath the feeder.
He lolls in tall grass, stretches his belly
against cool green earth, only eyes
and ear tips visible.
Occasionally the dog catches a scent
eagerly sniffs erratic patterns
across the lawn; rabbit is long gone
watches from the perimeter.
One tentative step
and he bullets under the fence
or deep into tangled bramble that hides
his nest. Eventually the dog tires,
returns to the house.

But at night, when the old dog
sprawls on his rug beside the bed
breathing wheezy and regular
he chases rabbits in his dreams
paws twitching rapidly
nails click, clicking the baseboard.

Paret, Widowed

Lids seal by vacuum pull,
      only the rims to be tightened
           come morning.
She'll nestle them among jars of shine.
No one around to see her
      place two dozen neat jars of piccalilli
           on the sideboard.
No one to see her
      wipe her brow on apron hem
           day's heat still clinging.

She plunges hands beneath the tap
      holds them there
           savoring rush of cool water,
dries them on her apron,
      reaches for the lotion
           she keeps beside the sink.
They are an old woman's hands:
      nails ridged, so thickened
           she trims them with a knife.
How odd, when her skin grows thin,
      translucence revealing veins
           as blue calligraphy.

She trudges to the bedroom,
      consigns her blue gingham,
           to the hall tree Auty fashioned
steam-bending the ash.
      Settling herself before the mirror
           she unpins her hair.
Stars tonight seem within reach.
      In the stillness, she listens
           for the repeated low cough
of a two-cylinder engine—

something illicit, running, no doubt,
without lights.
Justice and legality are not necessarily
the same; now she finds that
necessity trumps both.

Terrance

He pedals gravel shoulders: county roads,
rutted lanes. Sometimes over the bridge,
down the island. Sometimes north
to the state highway. Along marshes,
through parking lots, he gathers bottles
in a basket wired to his handlebars;
two more flank his back wheel.

It's a girls bike—today the red one—
but he doesn't mind, pulls his cap low
above his eyes. Jeans. Hi-tops. Striped shirt.

Children wave and shout, *Hi, Terrance.*
He waves back. If he bends a spoke
or has a flat, someone stops,
tucks his bike in the car, drives him home.

Terrance returned this way from war.
He collects pop bottles—it's his job—
returns them, spends the change
on beer at the bar. Like other men.

Ziggy and the Git Warm

He called him *Ziggy,*
don't know why.
Had names for all his grandkids:
Possum, Humbug, Ladybird.
They just budded on his tongue.

Ziggy was his favorite
though he didn't show favor
bounced 'em all on his knee, sang
Animal Fair and *Bicycle Built for Two.*
Took the boys for first haircuts.

Ziggy grew tall, broad-shouldered
not skittish about hard work
when there was hard work to be done
and salt water ran in his veins.
At fourteen, he knew the tides,
read the weather, walked on sea legs.

Up 5 AM of a summer morning
he'd cull the trot line—
knew a *jimmy* from a *sook*
three feet below the surface.
Out on open water as sun cracked the sky
and mist billowed from a glassy surface—
chill even in June, July.

Then Papaw'd say, *Ziggy,*
where's that git warm?
and he'd clamber forward
pull the bottle from behind coiled rope.
Papaw would take a pull or two
offer Ziggy a little pull as well.
Feller doin' man's work

gits treated like a man.

Years later, as Ziggy wandered
job to job glossin' n scrappin' along
rooming house to shelter to jail
losing his license, losing his way…
Did Papaw, retired to his easy chair,
take on any blame? Had he not offered
that first golden burn
at the back of the throat,
would the git warm still
have called Ziggy's name.

The Night Clerk

at Severn Inn
slips out for a cigarette;
wrinkles in her tunic match
the ones around her eyes.
She turned forty last week,
and two of the staff threw a party.
There was music. There was revelry.
There was wine.
She drank enough to moon
her shift manager.

Tonight, she's hung-over
again, fighting to stay awake,
sipping stale coffee
that eats at her belly.
She leans into the counter, wishes
the lights were not so bright,
so unforgiving. A young porter
strolls through the lobby,
whistles *Bad Moon Rising*.
When he grins at her,
she has the grace to blush.

Now That He Has Died

she moves to the mainland,
a neat white house above the river,
packs life in boxes: dishes, linens,
photos of children alive and dead.

Age rests on her shoulders,
but does not burden.

She unpacks records and cassettes,
from the forties on,
recalls a piñata she bought for Jason's ninth birthday:
paper machè burro, bright
with red, yellow and turquoise blue.

She hung it high;
children, blind and vicious with the broom,
left a shattered husk, dangling
paper streamers and cardboard innards.

For weeks foil-wrapped candies
sparkled in the shrubbery.

His House

Ridges of his calloused fingers
imprinted the mortar.
His sweat stained every 2 x 4.
He hammered every shiny nail
and eased each tongue into its waiting groove.
Two sunstrokes he had
shingling the roof's peak and pitch.
Wallboard raised by his hand,
was taped, spackled, painted green.
Years ago he carved risers for stairs,
hewed the oak mantle,
framed and hung the front door.
Neighbors watched him paint the flagpole,
sixty feet, telescoped in twenty foot sections.
And here on the doorframe is a burn
where a grandson played with matches.
And there is the door, hidden in paneling,
invisible entrance to eaves.
He wired his fence to keep cows from his garden,
removed wires when granddaughters toddled.

Now the house is empty,
furniture bequeathed or sold. It stands
among his flowers: rose, tulip, peony,
fills with strangers who have never woken
to doves among the eaves,
rushed to close windows against rain,
primed the pump following a storm.
They've paid well for this house,
rewired for computers,
drilled a new well for stronger pressure.
But his face reflects in every window.
At night when they snore in their beds,
this house still dreams of him.

102

Cap'n Auty

On a screened porch
he let me touch history:
explore a surgeon's-kit from the Civil War,
heft muzzle loaders, brass ship's lantern,
musket ball still clattering inside.

A practical man, when space grew scarce
he dumped it, burned it all.
Now, he lies in *wedding and funeral suit,*
longing for overalls, chambray shirt,
straw hat tipped low.

Susurrus washes papered walls, plush carpet,
scentless flowers. Nephews and grandsons
gather in open neck casual shirts,
blue-jeans, women in pants
and rubber sandals.

He'd disapprove, scowl at children
who race and squall,
lie appalled in that satin-lined casket—
(he'd never slept on satin his entire life!)
a bored and awkward guest
at his own funeral.

In the Kitchen of the Big White House

she forces grape pulp through cheesecloth
with purpled hands. I dreamed last night

of mice, pink rubber newborns. Folks say
to dream birth foretells death, so I eulogize:

She added long columns instantly
in her head. She paddled my mother

with a flyswatter, loved to eavesdrop
on the party line, sang loudly and off key.

She stole her sister's beau and eloped
to New York. She never cut her hair.

Blue-eyed and fair, she abhorred the sun.
Green was her favorite color. Merciless

at cards, she remembered who played each
one. When women got the vote she was first

to register, also to get a driver's license.
Never leaving the East Coast she traveled

the world through letters from pen pals,
rebaptized a foster daughter in her own

faith, adored men. She saved her best,
used her second best. Her canned peaches

won blue ribbons. She read newspapers
daily: front page, editorials, obituaries,

Mutt and Jeff. She was never without
her ubiquitous apron, hair bound in a bun.

Brothers call her a velvet bulldozer;
she is an intricate puzzle box.

Miss Frankie

She passes the window,
stooped, shuffling in flickering lamplight,
pacing when restless legs allow no sleep.
The world quiets
as if all life is suspended.
Her slippered feet wear dull paths
like sky maps
tracing a lonely planet's orbit.

A heart monitor strapped to her side
is baggage she must bear,
but she won't relinquish the cigarette
dangling from her lip.
She's buried two husbands,
five of eight boys.
She paces, pauses,
slaps card on card in endless solitaire.
Almost blind, almost deaf,
she pulls the TV nearer her chair,
turns it up again.
Too much trouble to wear her teeth.

But, one son brings mail, removes trash,
and one delivers groceries:
microwave entrees, bread, milk,
an occasional garden tomato,
and sugar wafers—*Lordy,* she says,
I do love them sugar wafers.
Damn doctors don't help none, she reports.
Talking on the phone plumb wears me out.
It's been a good life, but
if the Good Lord wants me, I'm ready.

Miss Ruta

An old stewing hen, tough and stringy
as chickens she raised. Brown and dusty
as she spread her wash over bushes to dry,
picked grapes, gathered crab apples,
blackberries or wild asparagus. As she split wood
for the cast-iron cook stove and pot-bellied Franklin
that heated the parlor. As she placed buckets and pots
at strategic points to catch drips when it rained.
Busy all day, she smelled faintly of corn
from dresses made of feed sacks. A hand pump
mounted at the sink provided water—it was enough.
But a new outhouse yards from the door
was convenience.

Widow, healer, seer, staunch Roman Catholic
and witch, she could make a poultice of coon fat
and wintergreen to draw poison from a chest
as easy as she could bake a rhubarb slump or turn out
eighteen perfect jars of cherry preserves. Cancer
took her in her eighty-seventh year—long months
of grueling trips to the county seat where fluid
was drawn from a swollen belly. After she was gone
her daughter found twenty dollar bills
slipped between pages of a book, under a rug,
wadded in an old coffeepot, empty purse,
back corner of a drawer—always a little money
tucked away to meet the unexpected.

Church Dinner: Labor Day

Susie slips between long tables, refills
sweet tea. Conversation's cicada buzz;
ice clinking—everyone nods or smiles. People
pack elbow to elbow, fans waft scent,
provide little relief—every window propped.

Crusty men in pressed slacks greet others,
shirts stuck to sweaty backs: *Hot enough?*
Stockingless ladies flush pink in Sunday clothes,
flutter funeral home fans, glow, don't sweat.
Deed, did he! they cry, and *Lordy. Lordy.*

Bowls of green beans, sliced tomatoes,
cob corn pass. Miss Birdie runs the bake sale:
cakes and pies, whole or by the slice. Men
jostle for position: Miss Nora's Baltimore cake,
Miss Libby's sweet tater pie.

Susie replenishes a crab cake platter;
Uncle Birch helps himself, shakes his head,
blames dwindling catch on...*red tide,*
pollution upriver, that oil storage place.
No waterman blames over-harvesting.
Till nary a one's left, he warns.

Empty dishes. Crumbs. Spills. Women
wash up as evening rolls off the water.
Children play freeze tag, swinging statues,
catch lightning bugs while men light pipes
and cigarettes, pass a flask. *Nary a one left,*
they repeat sadly, *nary a one.*

Family Graveyard

Narrow right-of-way
rambles through wild cherry trees,
small fruit ripened to deep purple.
Split rail fence,
time-silvered, lichen-stained,
encloses a little square
scarcely larger than my living room.
Windfalls spatter headstones
with blood, engraving so faint,
so shallow, I can barely trace it
with a finger. Grandma, Grandpa,
Mama, Althea, Baby Anne,
sleep beneath stones
tilted, sinking,
blasted by hurricane and nor'easter.
They lie west to east
within purview of the river
as it nibbles the banks—
water level higher each year.

About the Author

Ann Howells was born, raised, and educated in the Chesapeake Bay area of Maryland. She moved to Texas in 1979. In 1990 she joined Dallas Poets Community, a workshop and service group, and served on its board through 2018. She joined the staff of *Illya's Honey* poetry journal, becoming its editor in 1999. In 2012, she moved the journal from print to digital format and took on a co-editor. (www.IllyasHoney.com). The journal finally closed its doors in 2017.

Ann presents frequently at literary conferences and festivals and is often solicited to serve on advisory boards and panels and to judge poetry competitions. She is particularly fond of working with students and conducts workshops and readings in schools, elementary through college. In 2001, she was named a "Distinguished Poet of Dallas" by the city. Her books include *Under a Lone Star* (Village Books Press, 2016) which was illustrated by Dallas artist, J. Darrell Kirkley, and *Cattlemen & Cadillacs,* an anthology of Dallas/Fort Worth poets which she edited (Dallas Poets Community Press, 2016). She read her work and was interviewed on the television show, *Writers Around Annapolis* in connection with the first of her four chapbooks, *Black Crow in Flight* (Main Street Rag, Editor's Choice 2007).

Another chapbook, *Softly Beating Wings* (Blackbead Books, 2017), was published as the winner of that year's William D. Barney Memorial Chapbook Competition. Her poetry appears widely in small press and university publications here and abroad, including *Spillway, Little Patuxent Review,* and *Calyx* in this country, *Magma* in England, and *Crannog* in Ireland. She has been seven times nominated for a Pushcart.

Ann lives in Dallas with her husband, daughter, and two dogs. She is a voracious reader, not only of poetry but of novels, particularly Scottish noir. Three things you may not know about her: she still uses a flip phone, she has wind chimes in her car, and she has been known to go into withdrawal after three days without Mexican food.

www.ingramcontent.com/pod-product-compliance
Lightning Source LLC
Chambersburg PA
CBHW032105080426
42733CB00006B/433